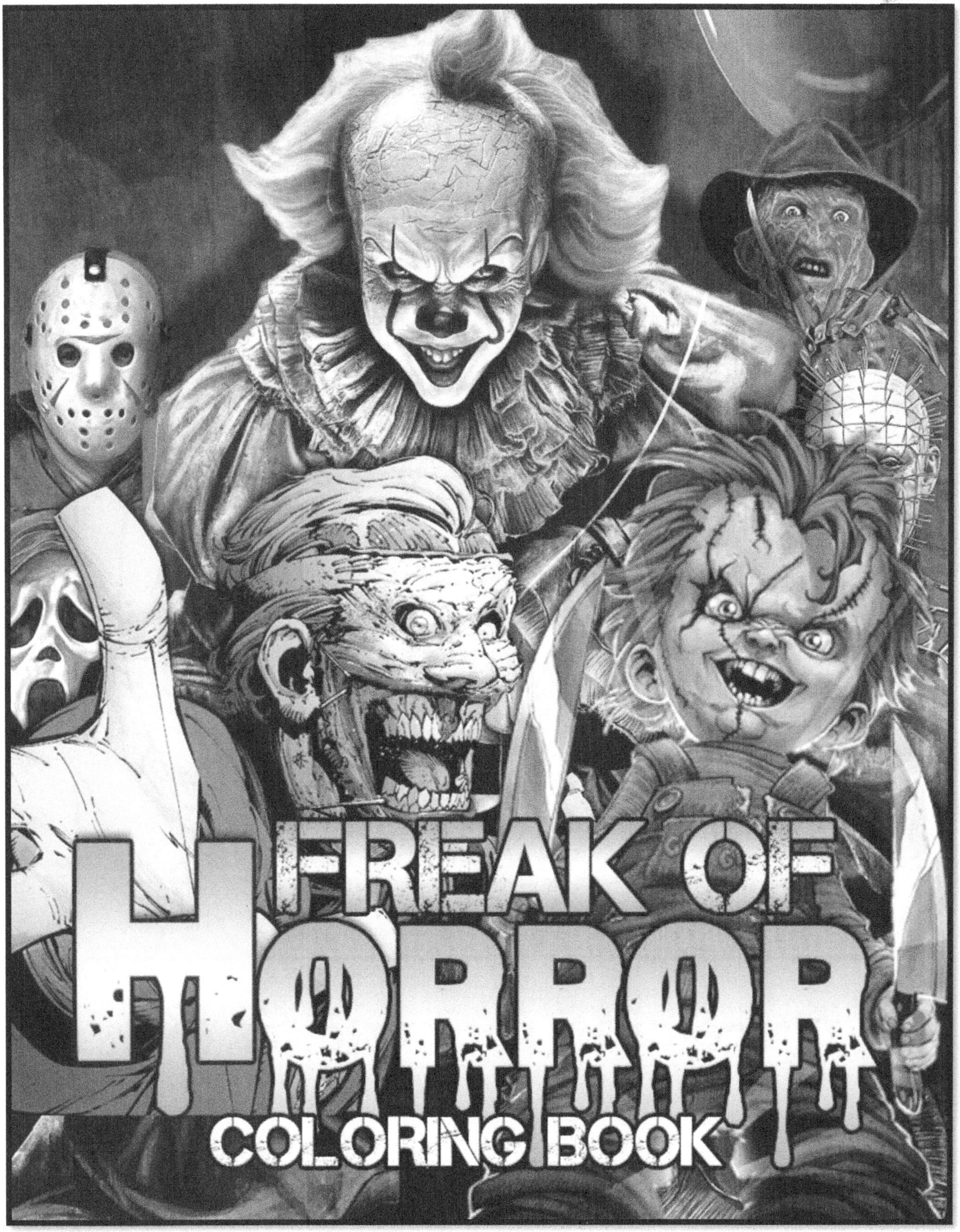
FREAK OF
HORROR
COLORING BOOK

THIS COLORING BOOK BELONGS TO

COLOR TEST

PENNYWISE

MICHAEL
MYERS

JEFF THE KILLER

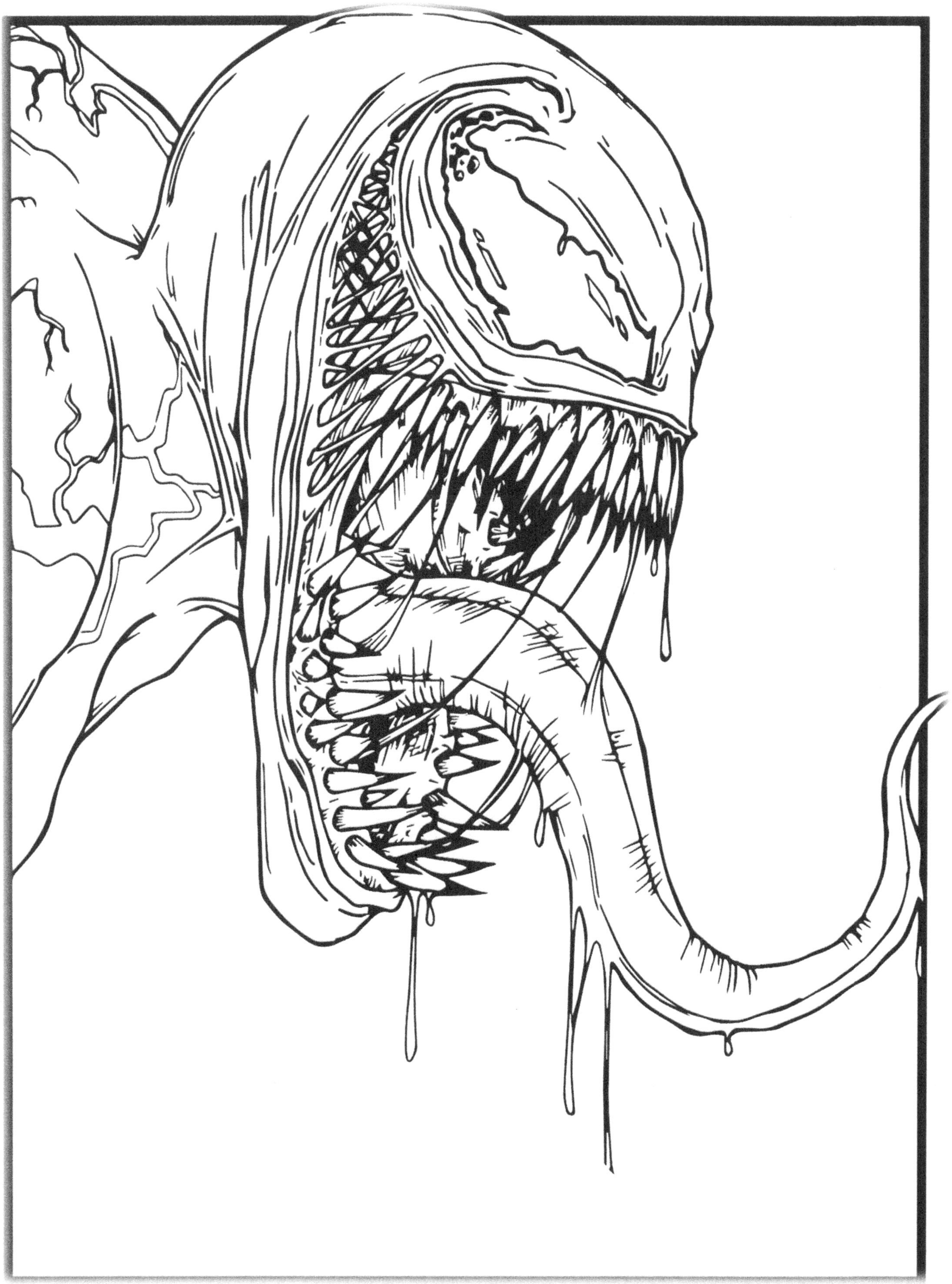

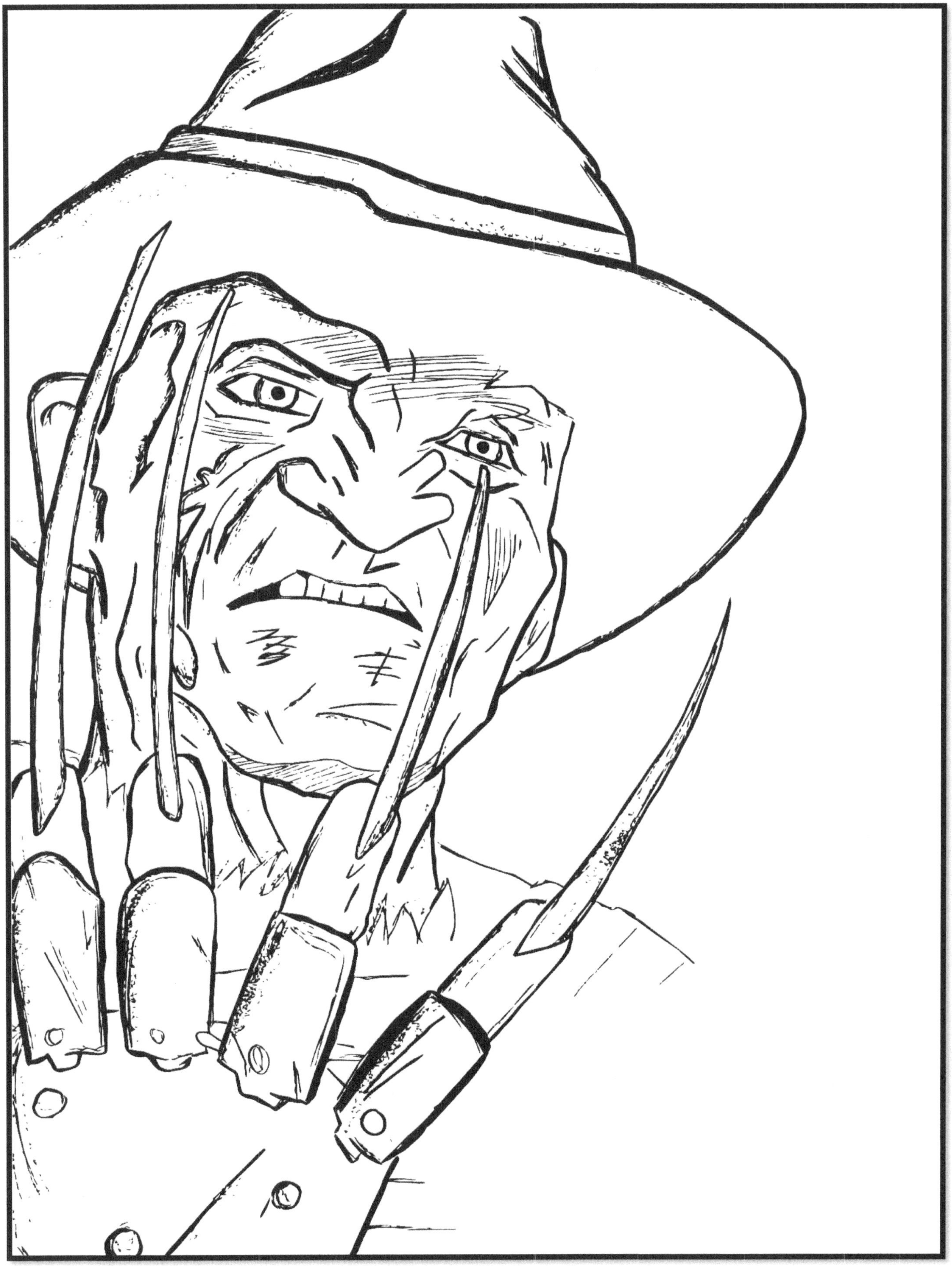

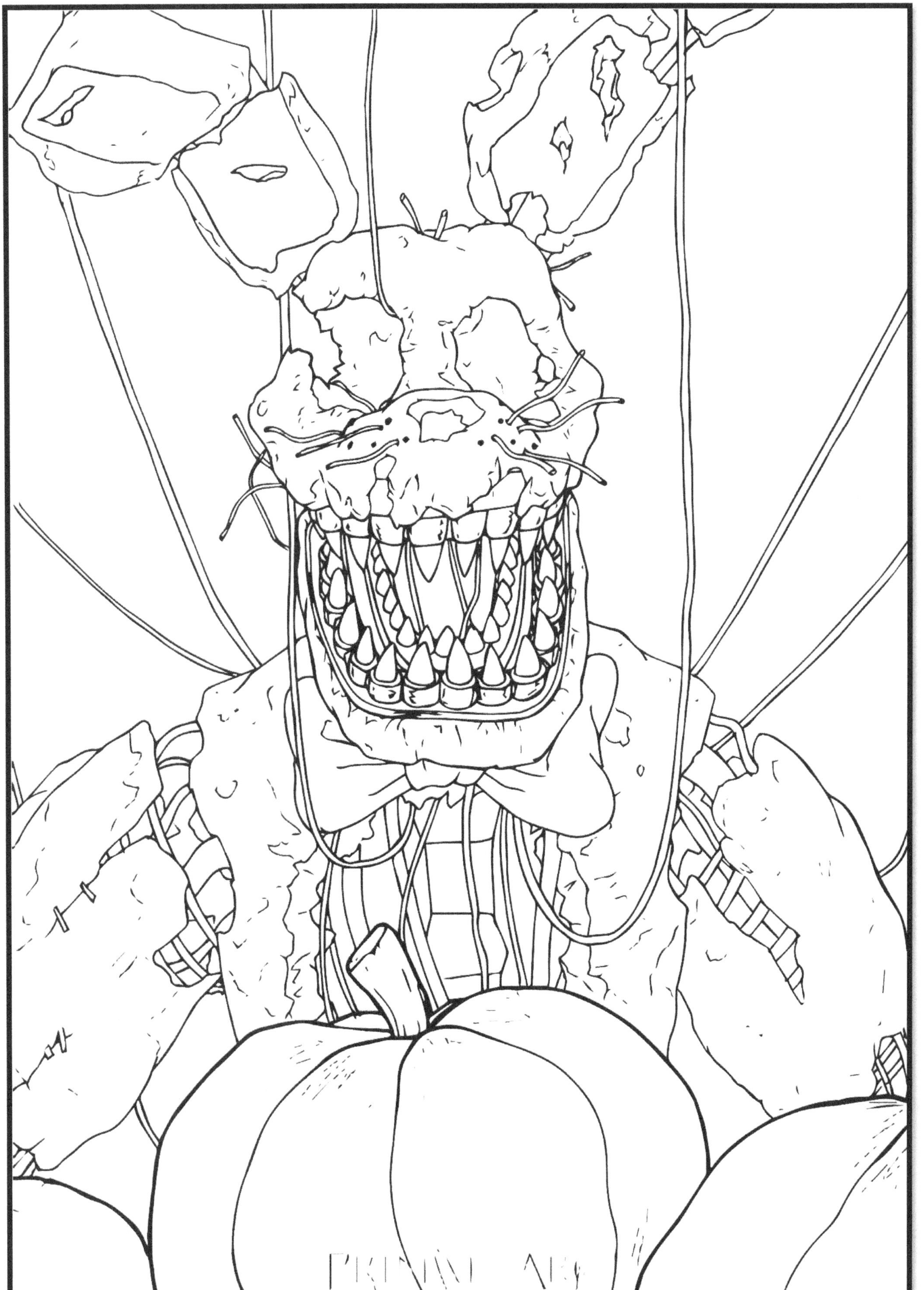

Sick

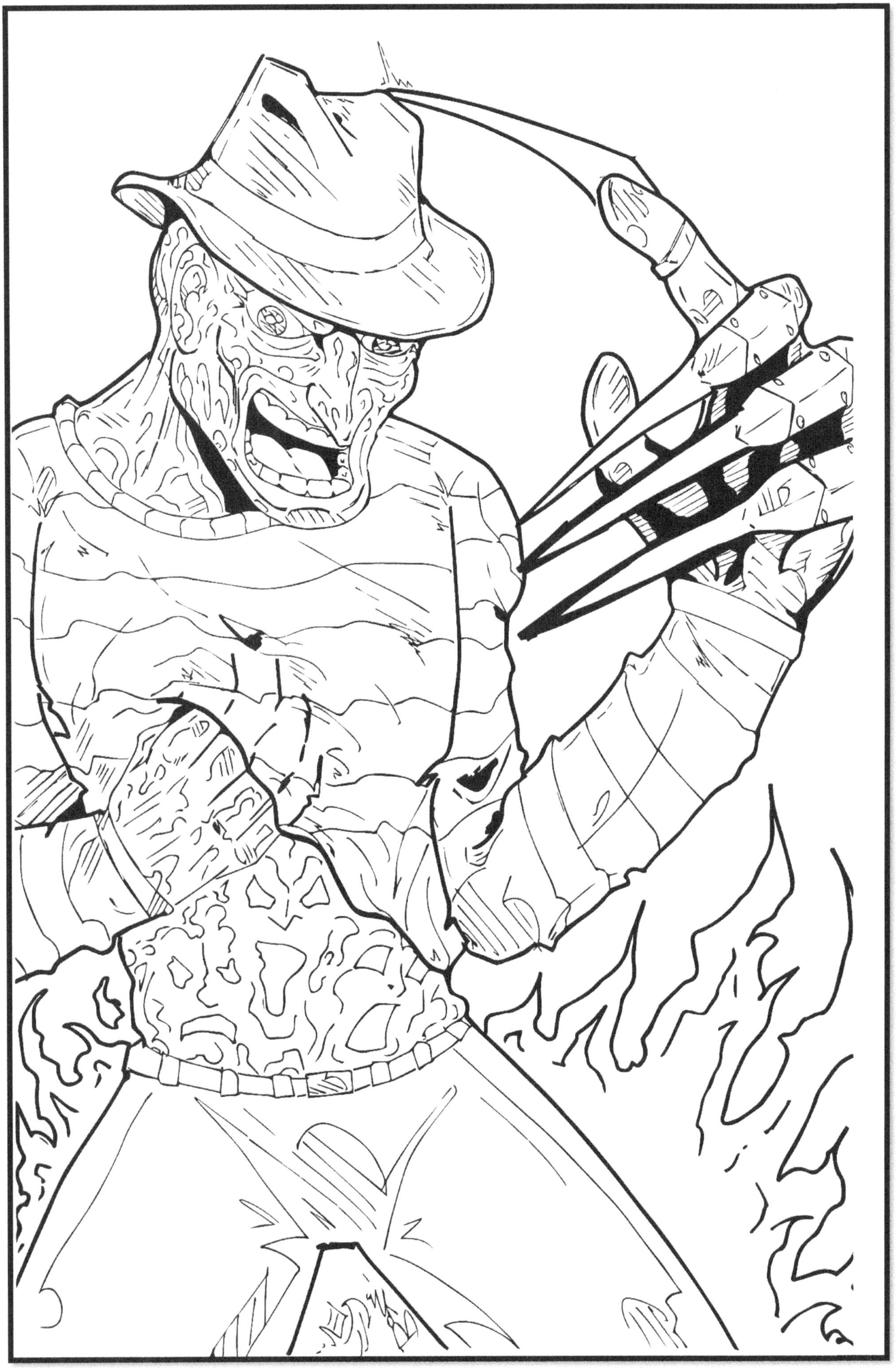

-POIS
WARNING

Demons

TRICK
OR
TREAT
HAHAHAHAHAHA
HAHAHAHAHAHAHA
HAHAHAHAHAHA

JASON
VOORHEES

Good

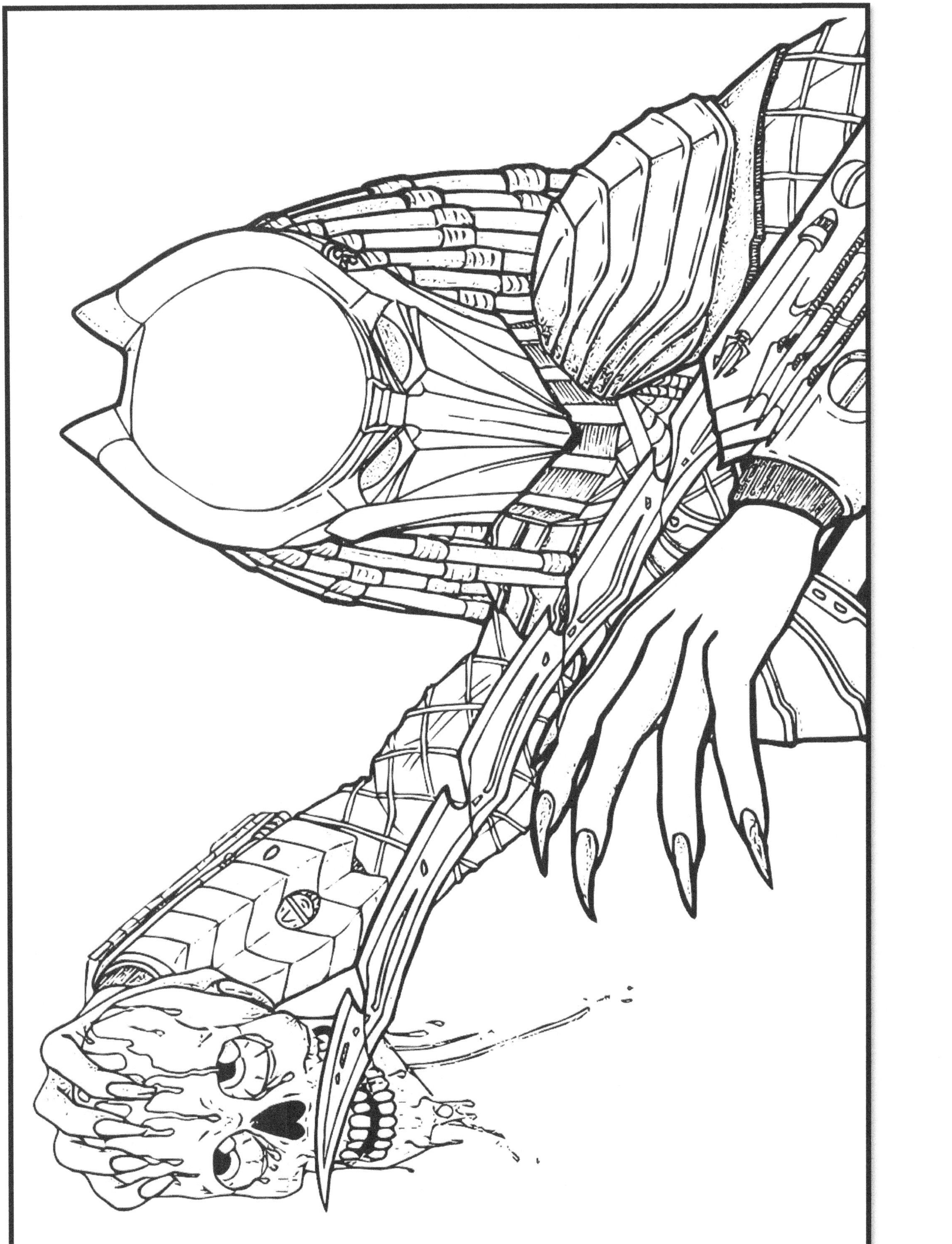

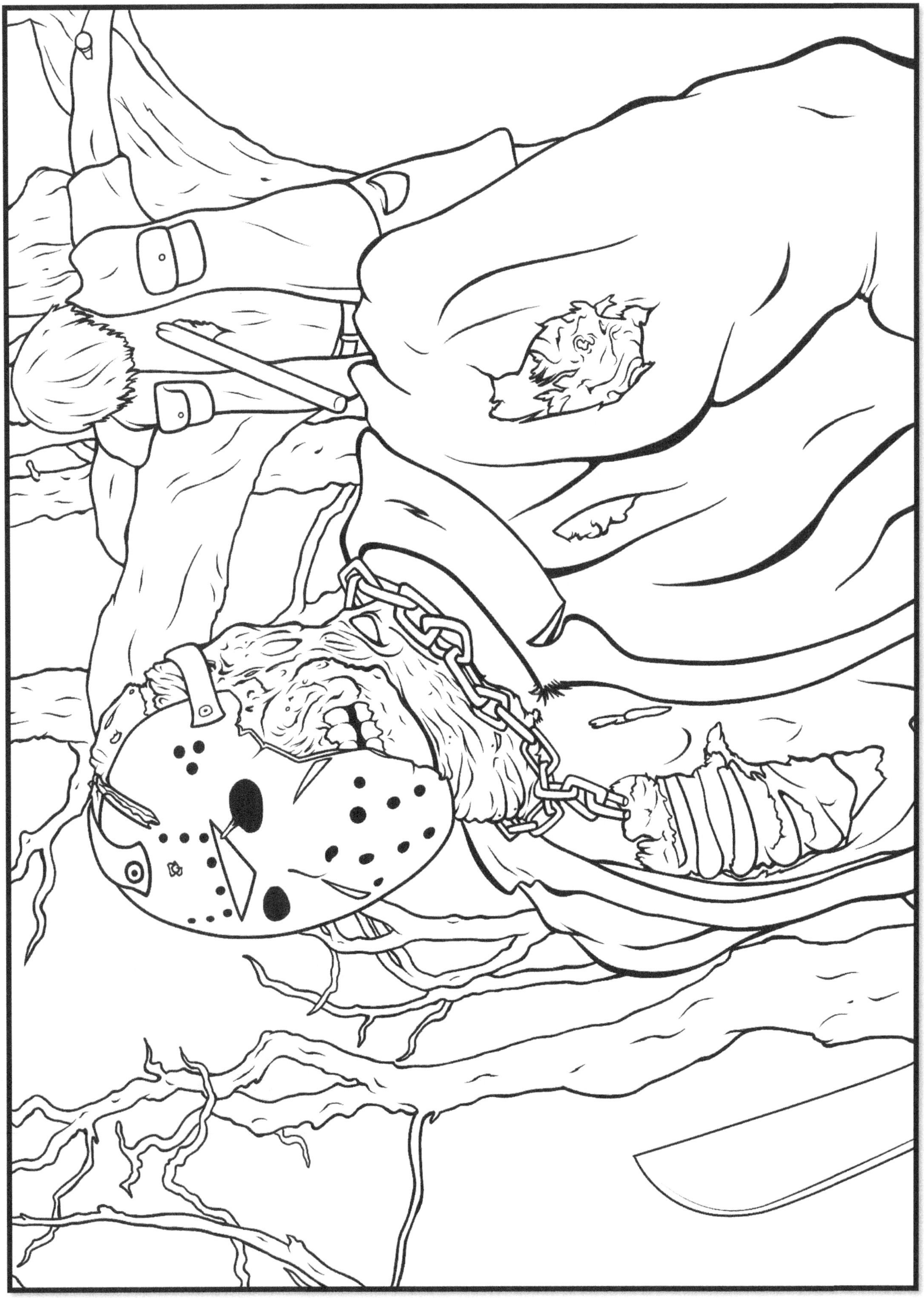

We hope you enjoy your purchase.

Don't miss to Leave us a review.

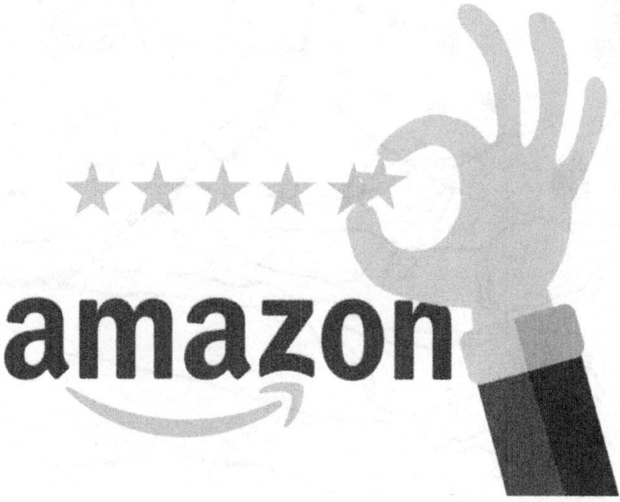